The Way of the Master
From innocent, to master of seduction

Master's Path

John Danen

Published by John Danen, 2023.

While every precaution has been taken in the preparation of this book, the publisher assumes no responsibility for errors or omissions, or for damages resulting from the use of the information contained herein.

MASTER'S PATH

First edition. October 10, 2023.

ISBN: 979-8224201969

Written by John Danen.

Table of Contents

Introduction.

Getting to the top is not easy at all, in fact, it is extremely difficult. You go through countless problems and terrible moments where everything looks black, so black that you even give up thinking that it is not possible.

In this book I will relate how to reach success based on my personal adventure to get to where I got to, which although it is not a brutal success, I do consider it a success. I will not only tell the successes, but also the failures, the b-side, the hard learning, because every time you make a mistake there is a learning process, and also by failing you advance and after much practice, you become a master.

The big teaching of the whole book is that you have to be a fighter, a guy who takes the hits, gets up and keeps going. A guy who has Enormous ambition and is almost always dissatisfied with his performance, a guy who is willing to keep going no matter what he suffers. A guy who does that can go the distance.

In the book "How to materialize what you want with the fxxxxxx Power" I explain in detail and in an impersonal way the steps to follow to reach success, in this book I will tell you what has been my whole journey, the good and bad moments I have gone through. I will give you the keys and the skills to be acquired, extracting the lessons from each situation experienced. I hope it will inspire you to walk your own path and get to where you want to go, hopefully a very high place.

The rawness of life.

That's right, life is terribly crude. Almost no one reaches something decent, many do not even have a project, those who are the vast majority, do not get anywhere, because they have a default life, which is the one assigned to them by the system. Among those who have a clear vision of where they want to go, some, those who put firm determination to transform their current life into their ideal life, get there.

Time goes by and many times your abilities diminish, your strength weakens. Of course you have no support from anyone, neither from family nor from friends. Nobody will understand that you want to be a great flirt, a seducer. They will see it badly or at least they will think - This man is crazy! So how no one will understand you or help you, the only one you have is yourself and it is you who you have to follow and who you have to please.

Whoever does not have firm determination, whoever is not capable of sacrificing much of his life for this cause, whoever cannot focus on this, whoever is not capable of an immense, hard and absorbing dedication, fails completely.

The failed ones.

Many people have surrendered to the system without even being aware that they have not projected a way of life for themselves, that they have been living a life by default without aspiring to anything. If you do not have a successful self-concept of yourself and ambition to achieve, you will reach nothing but utter mediocrity in your life.

People die without having lived, without having achieved what they wanted, without having developed their potential.

They are recognized because they wander, but they do not walk. They wander aimlessly in life from here to there without a clear plan. In their heads they feel life as a hostile place where survival is enough, and they only aspire to that. To a life by default, to a common job, a common girlfriend, an economy that gives them to live without many luxuries. If they do not suffer hardship, that is enough. The work they do will always be for others, that is to say, they will work for others, because they do not have the courage and the vision to start their own business.

Having a bad economic area will have repercussions on your self-esteem and will spoil the other areas. Only a few will be able to seduce with this area badly, the really good ones.

Seduction is even more difficult than the economic area. That's why most of them don't even try.

But there are some who do have what it takes, a monstrous dedication, a failure-proof self-concept, an inner belief that they are attractive. Those few who are born very handsome and are in demand just for this, and above all, those who develop their attractiveness by their enormous desire to seduce girls and are willing to sacrifice whatever it takes and put in the enormous dedication that is necessary, these few will show the way to others and do things impossible for everyone else. Things envied to the max like being with lots of beautiful girls.

For me all the others are the losers, the ones who don't make it, the ones who no matter how much money they make are not envied at all, because the women they have are not seduced by them, but by their money. We seducers are the winners and everyone else the losers.

The way of the master.

The path of the master is an incredibly hard path. The funny thing about this path is that when you start it you are not even aware that you are starting it, because usually your goals are not to become a master in seduction, you simply want to improve. This path is usually taken at the age of 12, 14, or 16.

I think there are people who are incapable of taking this path, people who reject it intellectually considering it a bad thing. People who do not want to become masters in seduction at all. Others start this path without realizing it, because what is a small thing today, will be the starting point for great things tomorrow, so you usually don't know very well when you start walking it.

What I do know is what has happened to me, so this I can tell. I can also give my opinion of how others take the path.

I believe that the path of the teacher begins in a very remote place in time, when you are still a child and you start to notice girls and to like them. This can happen between the ages of 10 and 12, being already at thirteen something imperative. The path of the master begins one day in late childhood, when you are neither a child nor a teenager, you are something in between. On that day you begin to develop this attraction to women.

In my case, I think I started this path in my childhood, because I always liked girls. Being a little boy, there were girls that I thought were very pretty, and with whom I imagined situations where I was their hero, I protected them and I was with them; even without knowing very well what to do. In my imagination I was close to them, in physical contact and they admired me, they looked at me a lot and I felt loved. This is how the teacher's path begins. In the imagination of a boy who feels attracted to girls and wants to like them.

So practically everybody started this path, because I am sure that this is something that many, many people imagined and felt. Practically everybody started the path, but almost none of them walked it completely.

Others start on this path later, as I do not know how each one's head is, I will tell you what I experienced.

Childhood.

As I said before, since I was very young I liked girls, and it seems that I had a certain magnetism and they also liked me, at least a little bit. I remember when I was four or five years old my mother used to take me out to the terrace to eat. Across the street on the nearby balcony lived two girls named Marián and Beatriz, and when I went out to eat they saw me and asked their mother to go out too. I was talking with them laughing and having a good time and thanks to this those girls were also eating their food looking at me. Their grandmother said that whenever I went out to eat on the terrace the girls were entertained and ate.

It is also true that I was quite funny and witty and I was friendly and talkative, I knew how to make people laugh, I imitated people and things like that that made me quite popular. But this was when I was older, not there on the terrace.

When I was about six years old, these friends told the girl I liked that I liked her, this made me feel terrible and I was crying because they made me feel very ashamed telling her this. Besides there were eight or ten girls all saying this in front of her, so maybe I was a little traumatized, but it wasn't something very serious I think.

The next important thing in dealing with girls was when I was about 9 years old, when my friends took me to chase a girl and call her pretty, I didn't like it but I did it to go with them. This was an older girl of about 12, much older than us. The girl's nostrils were swollen and she turned against us and grabbed me, who was the most innocent one, and, by surprise, slapped me in the face, which left me dead. This was a trauma because I forgot it for many years and I remembered it one day when I was 31. Maybe this was what upset me a little against them. And so, without knowing it, the basis for being a bad boy was laid inside me, because this was forgotten there but affecting the inside. I think that at the beginning I became afraid of them and then this turned into contempt. I think that everything that happens is for a reason, so God wanted me to have that resentment inside without knowing it, which little by little came out in arrogant pimp behaviors that gave me so many victories.

At 31 the whole trauma must have come out and things were already balanced in terms of bad behavior on each side so I could remember it.

And so, doing more harm than good, I repaid them for the harm done.

When I was twelve years old there was a girl I liked, there was always someone I liked and of course I did not dare to talk to her, I was shy and insecure because of this trauma and I was not able to do anything special, I was a textbook fool. I was about to give this girl a kiss on the mouth when I was 12 years old, just by asking her. She said yes, but when she stood in front of me, I didn't know what to do to her and I chickened out and didn't do anything to her.

Then at thirteen having regretted the whole fucking year the uselessness done the year before, I went back to the charge and tried with that same one again, and this time I did give it to her, and it tasted like glory. It was my first tongue kiss and it changed me and made me feel more like a winner. It was the summer of 1983.

Acquired qualities:

- Desire to redeem yourself from your past mistakes. This is simply a desire to improve.
- Dare to interact.
- Have the courage to ask.

Everything starts from a desire, from something with which you are not satisfied and that you want to improve, there begins the path of the master. As a result of that desire, of that not being satisfied, action arises, action badly done, but action after all. He who does not know how to create attraction, simply goes after them, being below them, and his only way to do something is to ask.

This is the most basic and simple and is often forgotten. The one who asks is directly accessing the closure. We often forget the most basic thing, ask. If you don't get what you want in a more sophisticated way, ask. Be the crying baby who cries at the breast. Ask and sometimes it will be given to you. If you don't try and don't ask, you're not doing well.

Everything was to be done. At least with these qualities you are making progress by beating yourself up. This is better than doing nothing.

- Wishes to improve.
- Interact
- Requests.

With this kiss my childhood ended and adolescence began.

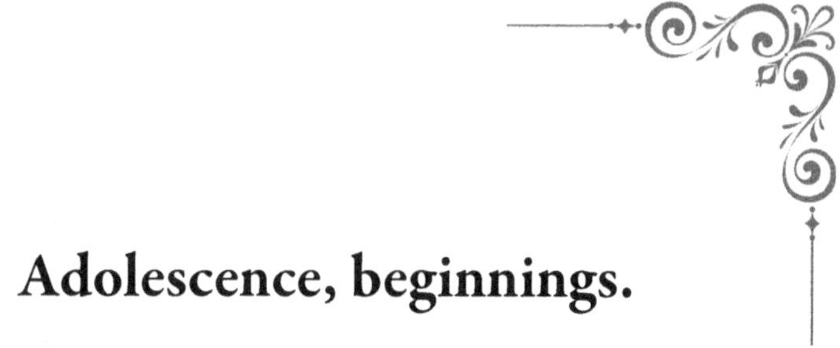

Adolescence, beginnings.

Thanks to this apprenticeship I had the most basic weapons to keep on adding. So one day in my summer resort the following year, 1984, I told another girl that I wanted to give her a kiss and she said yes, and I gave it to her. But with such unsophisticated weapons little could be done, and I lacked another important quality, which was to dare to use them.

The following year, 1985, I didn't have that nerve and despite meeting countless girls, I didn't have the balls to say this to any of them. So little was done in this time of apprenticeship.

The next improvement was to use your weapons and I didn't use them.

This was a hard period, hard, no, very hard. To the immense desire to kiss girls and do things with them was added a tremendous sexual need, which made you be at their mercy, you thought a lot about them, you were needy and dependent to the maximum, you were sexually super frustrated and you didn't know anything about anything. A time that was hard, but as you did not know anything else, it seemed good to you, because you had the illusion of moving forward and you enjoyed every interaction.

People were gradually waking up and you saw how one did something with one, another with another, another with several. You practiced and interacted at will, but you learned little, because you did not understand anything of what was happening.

I was nice and funny, I tried to make them laugh and I thought that they might like me, I used this so much that I ended up becoming the people's entertainer, the nice guy they look for to be at ease, but because of his absolute lack of mischief, naivety, innocence, and shyness, he was not able to attract any of them. If one was attracted, on top of being a pimp, I didn't consider her worthy of my attention, so I pursued some who rejected me, and rejected those who liked me.

At the very late 15 or early 16, I realized this mistake and decided not to over-please them as I had done before, by being a fun and cheerful boy, which is all very well, but not enough to please them, not having the malice of the bad boy, the one who makes them suffer with his wickedness and mischievousness. I realized this and applied it pretty well, but that wasn't nearly enough. I was soft, I liked them too much and thus seeing them as wonders I could achieve little.

In these years of 15 and 16 I learned not to please too much, to become more interesting and tougher. This was hard to learn but I learned it.

Another thing I learned is to consider myself a great handsome guy, to sometimes feel superior to them and this was worth it, but I only applied it to the ones I didn't like.

This time was not wasted, it was part of the learning process. This is how we reached the end of the 15 years with some important improvements.

The teachings of these years that you should put in your psyche are:

- Not to please them too much, not to play the clown, not to be available for them always pleasing them, so that later they would be taken away by other more badasses.
- Believe yourself to be a great beauty and like yourself.

Also, very little by little, I was beginning to detect the girls who liked me, this was easy, because of my great beauty there were many who liked me and I noticed it, and despite my immense flaws, they validated me to go out with them.

This, which was a great improvement, only uncovered the enormous internal shortcomings I had. I tell the story in the next chapter.

Adolescence. Clark Kent phase.

Well, yes, I was a very, very handsome guy at the age of 15 something, something spectacular, and that accelerated my relationship with girls, because they came to me, introduced themselves to me, wrote me love letters, and everything you can imagine.

I started to realize that physique matters a hell of a lot when you're really hot. And I was at tremendous levels. So, I told some of them that I would go out with them, and it became clear that behind my imposing physique there was nothing more than a cowardly boy.

I was afraid of them, I thought I didn't know how to kiss well, that I would make a fool of myself and they would laugh at me, that's why the first 4 times I went out with them I didn't do more than give them a little kiss on the mouth. In the end they got tired of having a fool and left me, which relieved me a little, because I lived every day with fear and stress, but also pissed me off terribly for feeling so silly. I blamed them instead of me for not helping me more for kissing them, and I became a bit spiteful.

This was because the second girl I kissed when I was 14 years old said that I did not know how to kiss, because of that I spent some time without daring to kiss any girl, as if that could not be learned. I made a fool of myself and I had to see how someone who went out with her hand in hand and was dating me and I did not kiss for cowardice, soon made out with someone much smarter than me. This was a fucking shit, but in the end it was excellent, because it gave me the bad temper to value them less and thanks to this, much later, to be able to pick them up en masse.

One day a high school classmate introduced me to some girls my age, they were smoking and looked very experienced, they intimidated me and I was very shy, I even stuttered because I was afraid of them. This was the bottom of my lost fool phase. I was in this phase because with that fear I had involuted and I was neither fun nor extroverted, but a little afraid of girls who seemed to be 10 years older than me, because I neither went out, nor smoked, nor drank.

I also attribute this involution to the overprotection of my parents, and to the changes of address, but above all to the first thing, to the fact that my parents did not let me do anything and kept me as a child. Fortunately, this horrible phase would end in a very short time.

I also once rejected a girl I liked and liked a lot and she liked me. This was due to being totally influenced by my mother who began to criticize and underestimate her. This girl was crazy about me and it was a real nonsense to reject her, because she was also very well off. It was a relationship of more than a year that got screwed up because I listened to my mother. She was the girl who was destined to be the number one girlfriend and I regret it! I regret not doing what I should have done. And this will never come back, the opportunity you turn down doesn't come back and you pay dearly for it later. This was punished with brutality after going through all those hardships that I would not have gone through if I had kissed her. If God gives it to you, you must take advantage of it.

The teaching of all this was:

- Physique, if it is brilliant, matters a lot.
- Girls are not going to take the initiative in kissing and practically in anything, you have to be the one to take the initiative.
- Being pissed off (for being so useless or whatever) is good, because it moves you forward.
- You must overcome your fears. To move forward you have to

face them, which I did not do, but that is the most important lesson of this era.

- Don't listen to your parents about everything.
- Never miss a good opportunity, for if you do, you will be severely punished.

Adolescence. Overcoming
the most ridiculous fears.

One day when I was 16 I met a classmate from high school who knew a girl from Valencia and wanted to introduce me to her. There I went and he introduced me to her, and I am grateful to him for that. He introduced me to her because she was from Valencia and since I had a lot of ties with Valencia, it occurred to him to introduce her to me. Surely she had seen or heard about me and this was the excuse to meet me.

I met her and little else happened that day. Another day I met this Valencian woman and she was with a friend. I was going to the disco that afternoon and this friend whose name was Isa was also going there, so I went with her.

That evening I flowed very well, I was uninhibited and I drank some cubalibres with this Isa in the disco.

I didn't value especially this Isa but I saw her as just another girl, neither good nor bad, so I wasn't intimidated, I didn't like her and I didn't think she was ugly, and I didn't feel anything special. And so without valuing her too much and uninhibited by alcohol we reached a good communication and ended up talking a lot, laughing and having a great time, and that inevitably, without wanting or planning it, led to spend the whole afternoon making out with her non-stop. I put on a good show and that day I overcame my ridiculous fears of kissing girls and stopped being a freak with them. Super late, by chance and without looking for it, but that's what happened. I had a fantastic evening. The Valencian girl found out about everything and that not only didn't hurt me, but it raised my status and in a short time she would also fall into my net.

This day I took another step on the path of the master, I stopped being a dumb geek and became simply a handsome fool. And being so handsome being dumb was enough to flirt a lot in those remote times.

So what do we learn here?

- We learn that if we don't value them highly we are more likely to like them.
- If we are uninhibited and fun we will attract them. Which was very easy because of the flow of the interaction.

As soon as I stopped thinking, I deactivated the brain and the limiting ideas that were crushing me and simply did what instinct was asking me to do, I did everything right and kissed the girl in the most natural way in the world. I didn't have to overcome any fear because in those moments I had no fear. It was as easy as that. I didn't think anything.

So don't think act.

Summarizing further:

- Don't value girls too much.
- Do not think about them or the interaction, or anything negative, thinking weakens your charisma. In the interaction just flow.
- Be fun and uninhibited.

First good deeds.

In Palma de Mallorca, at the age of 17, I was at the disco with hundreds of other teenagers from all over Spain. We were all going there to enjoy our excursions after finishing 3rd BUP.

On the dance floor, there was a stunning girl, she was the prettiest girl in the whole club. She was dancing around and around her there were at least 5 guys looking at her and clearly interested. I said 5 but maybe there were more, something like 7 or 8. I went up to one of them and said - fuck, she's hot! and he said - yeah man, she's awesome!

I stood there for a few seconds and it was very clear to me, I wasn't going to stand there like a moron admiring her, so without thinking about it at all, I had the balls to go talk to her, plus I was sure determined and super direct.

My presentation was something like.

-Hi, how hot you are, you look like the hottest girl in the club, I've seen you and I'd really like to meet you. She said

-Vale-

I told him

-Let's get off the track.

She came with me to the envy of the whole fucking disco, the admirers were there fucked that they had not been the brave ones, and we went to stand next to a padded column and there in a very short time, or I told her that I wanted to kiss her, or she already told me directly, or it was done easily without saying much. Besides, she looked happy, as happy as I was to be with me. And that night I was making out with a very hot girl to the envy of all Mallorca.

After this exhibition many began to call me "the master" for such an action. And although I was in the paleolithic of seduction, with the pretty face and good body that I had, as soon as I asked for it, it was given to me. I used these weapons to do what I did, which was not a crazy thing, because there was no sex, but it raised my self-esteem a lot.

Teaching.

- Have confidence in yourself and show them even if they are impressive, many times no one dares, and the one who does is rewarded a lot.
- If you are very handsome abuse this and with little you do it will be worth it and they will go with you.
- Isolate her, separate her from the place where she is, if she accepts this is that she likes you. I learned this by talking to another guy who at that time was just starting out and he taught me this trick. I learned it wonderfully and put it into practice that night for the first time.

Beauty.

By the time I was seventeen I was determined, and with the confidence that this great triumph gave me, I dedicated myself intensely to trying to pick up girls.

As a result of this dedication, I made a lot of friends with great ease, I really got into a higher gear, far above what the boys of my age were able to develop.

I would pick them up and then scorn them as if each one was to blame for something. I was a pissed off kid who wanted revenge for how bad I had it before when I was shy and good and they paid for it by abandoning me. Deep down I was still just that, a kid.

Now, more sure of myself, I began to stand out. Beauty gives you confidence, confidence gives you successes and these in turn give you more confidence. I didn't have to go in to many, just asking was enough, and sometimes it wasn't even necessary, they would come to me; they would introduce themselves to me, ask me out, or shout my name saying "hot guy" in the street. They would see me and their panties would fall down, they would say compliments to me, I practically had to do very little to pick them up.

I remember once at the disco I was introduced to a bunch of girls from a gang. There were so many of them talking at the same time wanting to meet me, that I couldn't attend to them all together because I didn't understand what they were saying, so I told them to make a queue so I could get to know each one well, and they made a queue of six or seven girls.

I used this technique of coming in, being nice and funny, and soon after telling them to come to a more intimate place with me. They would come over and I would be there kissing them all afternoon. At that time I had a great self-concept as a good guy, great enthusiasm and dedication and that paid off.

People don't necessarily have to start at the lowest level and go up level by level, they can go up faster, or start at higher levels. What you don't have is experience. The ranking I did in terms of seductive levels is based on experience and knowledge and not so much on results.

At this time I was dumb in knowledge, but I was not dumb in results due to the great advantage of beauty. I had many successes and the results were not at all foolish, but rather very smart. For the age I was super smart, as no one did practically anything, kissing girls in that remote era was considered by all to be masterly.

We are talking about the 80's in Spain, besides, I lived in a very traditional city, where people were often given 20 or 22 without any experience. This was not America where some people at 13 or 14 were even sleeping with girls.

Having the self-concept as "the most handsome" I could enter any girl without fear. And not only did they pay attention to me, but some of them didn't believe that they had been chosen, because they considered themselves very inferior to me. This gave me a lot of confidence. If you have this advantage you have to use it, if you don't, create a competitive advantage in your head. Feeling above the rest, I even picked up the hottest girls in town with great ease.

I had this competitive advantage and this accelerated the learning process. Thanks to this, progress was made much faster.

Previously at 14, 15 and 16 I was almost as handsome, but my shyness marred my beauty. Now at 17 I was exultant.

What can you learn from this?

- If you have a competitive advantage, abuse this advantage by getting it into your head and gaining the confidence to see yourself as a cut above the rest.

- If you do not have this competitive advantage, you must create it artificially with your thoughts. Thus, by repeating this advantage to yourself, by thinking about it and blindly believing that you really have this advantage, it will materialize in reality.

For example, you can believe that you are the most attractive, the toughest, or that you have something special that attracts girls, even if you are not handsome. This is much more difficult than the gifted life I had, where reality itself, without me thinking anything of it, told me loudly that I had that advantage.

You should also learn that the big handsome guys have no merit, because only for being handsome they get girls, and that sometimes behind their beauty there is no great wisdom or knowledge, since they are not even attractive, because behind their beauty they hide great insecurities, as it happened to me.

Being good looking in general is an advantage, but it is also a disadvantage, as you will develop very little charisma.

So if you are handsome you will have the advantage of being handsome, and if you are not so handsome, you will have the advantage that you will have to develop your mind more to make up for this deficiency. This not being handsome is not a disadvantage, it's an opportunity. Of course it's harder! and it's also harder, I know, it's much harder. At first it is a huge disadvantage, but always behind a disadvantage there is a huge opportunity. The opportunity in this case is that you will be forced to create an attractive personality. If you manage to create this attractive personality, this will be much more solid than the great beauty, which sometimes in a few years goes away, while creating an attractive personality creates a much more robust advantage and also remains for life.

The handsome if he does not develop anything else, as soon as he stops being handsome, he stops flirting. This happens because he tends to accommodate, he is not used to the no, to the rejection, to make an effort, he does not want to make an effort because for him it is insulting. Sometimes, because his ego is so high, he ends up not liking girls. Sometimes, they fall into depression as soon as that beauty diminishes. Some of them are already spoiled at 25 and fall down and do not recover. Also some handsome men who don't use their other weapons much, end up thinking that flirting is something of youth, and in their head as soon as they are no longer so young, they see themselves as old and finished. So what in principle is very good can be a disadvantage in the end, and what is very bad can become a huge advantage. In the end it all depends on you, on your head, much more than on your beauty.

In the end, creating an attractive personality is a more difficult path, but much more solid, lasting and meritorious, and this personality always ends up becoming a far superior weapon to beauty.

It should also be said that it is difficult for the handsome not to develop other weapons, because from so much interaction, and so much contact with girls, he learns more quickly how they are and how to like them, so if he starts to think and analyze things, the handsome can acquire wisdom very quickly.

If the handsome one is also smart, this will give him a definite and unattainable advantage for the rest at that moment. The handsome will reach very high levels very quickly. This beauty that gives him an advantage is not available to the normal, so his rise will be much slower as he builds up his attractive personality. It will take years to reach the performance of the handsome one. But don't worry, it will be slower but safer. The handsome one day will fall and even if it takes decades to reach his resume, this is a long-distance race, and in the end at 80 years is when you have to make the balance.

Very often these handsome guys have a very short career, because they immediately find a beautiful girl with whom they fall in love and leave the seduction. As I said before, many do not get to develop other weapons, and if the beauty drops, they do not know how to return to the elite.

Enjoy your beauty if you have it, enjoy your ugliness if you have it, they are different weapons and both give you victory if you use them well.

Dedication.

Dedication will polish you and transform you into a seducer even with very little beauty. Use that weapon, suffer but persevere, in the end the handsome ones almost always stop flirting because they are handsome, and either they transform into attractive men, or they become extinct.

Dedication is a slow weapon, a weapon you will hate, a weapon at first far inferior to beauty, but it is a cumulative weapon, and little by little you will increase your power with it. Over the years you will flirt much more because of the experience gained with dedication, than because you are handsome. With dedication, persisting, being tireless, in the end you will beat all the handsome men, you will laugh at them and you will see them in the distance, you will see them as remote memories of men who surpassed you and who today are no one, because they have been buried by oceans of time, and above all, of women you enjoyed. You will end up seeing them far, far below you, and you will end up feeling sorry for them.

Celebrate that the handsome ones surpass you, at least you have rivals, if you follow the master's path to the end, at the summit, you will be totally alone.

What we learn from all this.

- That dedication is our slowest but in the long run our best weapon, because by dedicating yourself and dedicating yourself, little by little you realize what you do right and what you do wrong, you polish your personality, you gain experience and finally you become a great flirt without the need to be handsome.

You are your only rival.

Another step on your master's path is this, to realize that you are your only rival.

Stop comparing yourself with others, of feeling better or worse depending on whether you look better or worse than others. If you go with fools you will stand out and feel the smartest, but you will really be fooling yourself. If you go with super smart you'll think you're dumb, when maybe what you are is one of the smartest in the place. So stop comparing yourself.

The one you have to compare yourself with is yourself, and not with the best you have done so far, but with the best you think you can be. This comparison will bring you back to the sad reality that you are doing practically nothing compared to the perfect circumstances and your maximum imaginable performance.

You should not martyr yourself for not being at your maximums, but be aware of the infinite margin for improvement that remains. The path of the master is a long, winding road, with maximum dangers and difficulties. Only if you are determined will you reach the end.

What do we learn here?

- That life is a struggle against your insecurities, fears and shortcomings. This struggle is the one you must undertake all your life, everything external being a manifestation of your victory or defeat in this field.

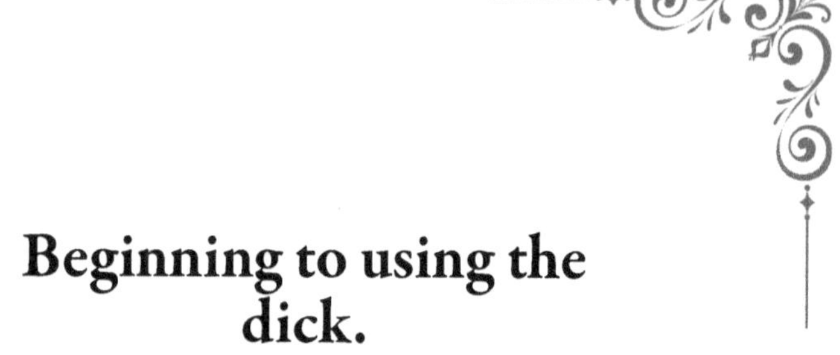

Beginning to using the dick.

So far in the way of the master there were only mental improvements, a few kisses and little more, now came a time when I realized that all that did not satisfy me at all and I wanted much more. I wanted to have sex with the girls I was picking up, and the truth is that they were super wasted, because I wasn't doing much. To some I touched a tit, to another I touched her pussy, but superficially, because she did not let me get to the lips, and anyway, I was advancing of course, but I still had not had sex at nineteen years of age. A very late age for what is normal nowadays.

But one night flirting even without wanting to I began my journey in this field. It was with a foreign girl in the summer resort. With this experience I understood that I could not let girls escape without having sex, that I had to at least try, I began to realize what I was missing out on because I was a fool.

At that time I had the limiting belief that in order to have sex you had to have a formal girlfriend, and hopefully she would let you do it after a long time, probably years. There were no books, no teachers, no internet, nobody had any fucking idea about sex or relationships. The only thing that schools, parents and society as a whole put in your head was that virginity was something very important, and I, used to hear derogatory comments about women who were not given to this virginity, thought that all women, except very few who were very poorly regarded, practiced it. The normal thing was to be a virgin until marriage and I thought I would be very lucky if I managed to do it before.

I thought that was the only way and that's where I was, because I got a girlfriend and things were going very, very slowly, and it seemed that it was going to take years to do it, if it was finally done.

With this girl that I hooked up with at the summer resort I realized that there were other girls who were more sexually liberated. Being a foreigner I thought that these facilities for sex were only applicable to very favorable circumstances, such as party places, and above all, to foreigners, and that they were hardly applicable to Spanish girls in their city of origin.

What do we learn from all this?

- We learn that the path of the master is a path that is full of obstacles, these obstacles are the limiting beliefs that you yourself have because you have been programmed that way. You are programmed to be foolish.

What else do we learn here?

- We also learn that thanks to dedication and practice, reality shows you that it is real and that it is not a fantasy you have in your head. Thanks to this dedication, at least I understood that there were favorable circumstances in which I could advance to the end.

If I had conformed to what was established I would have done nothing, and I would have remained a virgin until I was 23 or 24, as happened to almost all my high school classmates.

Limiting beliefs are also combated by performing the opposite action to that belief and observing the results. Many times you realize that what you believed to be true is not true, and thanks to this experimentation that disproves your belief, the belief is erased.

What I have told you here might make you think what a good-for-nothing! No matter, yes, it is true, I was a fool and I was trying hard enough to be as little foolish as possible. It was not easy to stop being a fool, not easy at all. In those days this progress from being a fool to less of a fool gave me great joy. You have to judge each one in his age, in his space and time.

The path of the master is hard, but it is also always a path to more knowledge and more power. Except when you enter at a very high age, where despite the enormous knowledge, you cannot materialize the power well because of the scarce market that exists, the path of the master is always to more knowledge and almost always to more power, because there are ups and downs according to the dedication and illusion of the moment, and motivating yourself, you can make memorable years at very advanced ages.

Immense failures that looked like impressive successes.

In the teacher's path there are immense successes that cause great happiness and in the long run: sorrow, pain, nostalgia, and above all a lot of lost learning time.

I met a girl who was very beautiful, very nice, adorable, touching. This girl gave me great love and absolute happiness. This same girl ended up becoming a tremendous obstacle for me on my way to the master because I fell in love head first, but, as life would have it, in the end I got tired and bored of this relationship.

Back when I was 18 years old I met a girl, as I said before, and I fell for Cupid's arrows. I fell in love and considered that I had already finished my minuscule love career, because I had found the love of my life. And so it was, it was the love of my life. No other woman would ever affect me as much or give me the happiness that this girl gave me. It was wonderful, I was excited, she totally corresponded me, everything was super nice, I never again had a girlfriend as loving and good as this one. So I totally retired from seduction very happy.

But, this happiness gradually vanished like smoke in the wind, and from wanting to be with her, my passion over time became to be with everyone but her, due to the disillusionment.

This girl became very monotonous and depressive. I started to realize that there were other girls out there much more interesting, and I resumed my pickup production even while I was with her.

What do we learn here?

- The more love we feel, the more pain we will have afterwards.
- That everything changes, nothing stays the same, generally things in love get worse, unless we make a huge effort, and even if we do.

Love kills.

On the path of the master, mistakes are made, and not because they have been made, but because they are not fixed and then things are always done right. No! Mistakes are made again and again even if you know things well, that is why this path is so hard, because you stumble many times with the same stone.

This stumbling is natural, because a nice and pretty girl really weakens, so it is natural to fall. These girls can and do stop your production quite a few times. Incredible as it may seem, they are also part of the way of the master.

You stumble upon love several times and are never fully immunized.

After this beautiful love comes a tiredness of it, then a happiness to return to the market even being involved in that love, and finally a breakup, that although you thought you were already strong and independent, it is harder than you thought; and many times you are very painful and sad even though it happened exactly what you wanted. This happens because you were softer than you thought.

On the path of the master, love is something that slows you down, weakens you, and makes you lose a lot of time. In the end it hurts and it leaves you terrible.

But if you never fall into it, nor do you know moments of great happiness, nor do you know real pain, so love hits you and you fall wounded, but after a few months, or more usually years, you get up and become you again. After a lot of suffering you find yourself again but this time much more hardened, tougher and determined not to fall into its terrible clutches anymore. This should always be the case, but sometimes you also look bad, feeling guilty and that will be catastrophic.

Love is the enemy of the seducer and only love and death can stop the production. Death stops it in its tracks, love slows it down but does not stop it, and soon, like dammed water that does not flow, the dam overflows, or breaks completely, and the river returns to its natural course.

What do we learn here?

- We learn that although love is very beautiful and something wonderful when you are in it, in the long run it ends up being a huge problem and you go from illusion to tedium. It is very hard to get out of it and get back to being yourself. You can fall into it several times, but you always get up and continue your production. The one who gets stuck never finishes the path of the master.

- The younger you are, I think the softer you are, because all the programming about romanticism, love, family, you have it more in your head. That's why I think many people commit suicide at very young ages like 15, 18, 21, when love seems to be the only important thing in life. Because of love many people have died, especially men. Love can kill you.

The false self.

In the path of the master there are moments of great wonders and mastery, and moments of absolute uselessness, fruit, as I always say, of the mental programming received. Actually, until you get to create your own personality and be you, you are really weighed down by all this shit that they put in your head, and practically, at least in my case, until I was almost 30 years old, I was not with my head in its place. You think you're the one who thinks and feels, but it's an artificial self that society created. Until you shed this false self, with false feelings and false tastes, you are not really you. This is not usually achieved until you have suffered harshly the consequences of the painful acts of this initial self.

Many people never manage to get rid of it, others manage to get rid of it around 30 because they have practiced a lot, most people are not themselves until they are 40 or 50.

In the end, almost always after a hard setback, the real you emerges and you discard all the harmful beliefs you had.

This tremendous weakness of this artificial self would cause me enormous problems.

In my case it happened that fortunately when you were going with your head that bad, it was not the girl who put me in my place, but life itself. You have already deviated so much from your master's path that the shock you receive is so great that you finally straighten up and go on the right path for the first time in your life.

Around 22 and 23 I got rid of this false self and was my successful creation, which was a marvel and what I am going to tell in the next chapter happened.

What do we learn here?

- If you want to succeed you must build a new, more powerful self, because the default self comes with incorrect programming.
- This change is positive, but if the old self surfaces it causes tremendous pain.

Stressful partners.

During the summers, already from 88, but especially from 92, when the organization of professional flirts was founded among the most savvy flirts there, a lot was learned and a lot was flirted, but it was really a very hard and very stressful apprenticeship.

At this time, I was already fed up with the girlfriend and I freed myself from fidelity. All the flirts and non-flirts met there in the summer resort, Benicasim. We, the flirts, those of the O.L.P. (Organization of Professional Flirts), we dedicated ourselves to flirt at all hours, in the morning, in the afternoon, at night, we went out practically every day. There wasn't a moment in which we weren't looking at a girl, or thinking about flirting with one. And so the summers went by.

The bad thing about all this was that, apart from this tension that you yourself had because of the enormous desire to flirt, your classmates did nothing more than stress you even more, because the competition was very big and anything wrong done, or any interaction that did not go well, was ridiculed and criticized by everyone. The successes you had were also ridiculed and criticized by some, so they gave ridiculing names not only to the ones I picked up, but to the ones anyone picked up.

"La morcilla", "la loca", "el monstruo", "Nenuco", "Elenana", those names were often given to very hot girls, like "la morcilla", who was called that way because she was dressed in black and was a very hot girl, but very hot. El Monster, because she was a big and tall aunt, Elenana, because her name was Elena and she was a bit of a dwarf, ha ha, I invented that one, things like that.

Sometimes we even hit on the same girls.

You had practically no one you could trust, for although you had some followers and allies who valued you as their leader, they were not very loyal, for they were not always there to go out with you, sometimes they changed sides depending on who was the strongest man, and the one who seemed your ally later allied with a rival.

I also have to say that 90% of the attacks came from a single person, the ringleader of the group, Pedro. He set up the group and was paid homage to by those at the lowest level. The matador and I were this man's challengers and we also ridiculed his many successes, as they were ephemeral and inconsistent. This was due to his poor ability to transform his flirts into girls he took to bed. This man kissed a lot of girls, but he slept with practically none of them.

The matador and I were allies and rivals at the same time and betrayals and great collaborations followed each other. In the summers when there was collaboration we both dethroned this leader, and in the summers when there was no such alliance they were not so good.

We competed to see who was the strongest of the three of us, we each had our followers and we were rivals with each other.

The summer of '92 clearly fell on my account and was thus recognized, as well as the summer of '93 tied with "el matador", both very evenly matched. In 94 I classified second, having allied myself with Pedro because the matador had taken a girlfriend and did not compete. With Pedro, in spite of everything, things were not so bad and we had a good summer. In 95 I was last because I was the one who got a girlfriend and I arrived in a very bad shape, fat and half in love. I was the worst not only among the three of us, but of all of us in a lousy summer. The 96 was a summer of betrayal of the matador who competed against me and beat me, I was third and well below, and 97 third again but closer to second.

So we were all there making alliances, breaking them and above all competing to see who was the most flirtatious. With this stress I did not perform well except for the first two years when I had many allies and followers, the rest due to the wear and tear of this war, I did not feel completely comfortable, and I could not give my best version.

As soon as I started to seduce on my own, stopping going with these people so competitive, stressful and of lousy companionship, I began to have many more successes. This was later, in my city, Santiago, from 97, there in Benicasim you could not go out alone, because it was very difficult to get away from all these despisers, traitors and rivals, because every night your supposed followers came to look for you, or directly your rivals. Sometimes you managed to go with someone less noxious and that's when you would hook up.

Normally within the group there were subgroups of two or three with a ringleader and one or more followers, you would find a friendlier partner who didn't annoy you and go with that one. The times you didn't have any allies to go with from among your followers or more like-minded guys, you had to go with your rivals and that used to be a shitty night where everything was tension.

That's how we were at the cockfight, screwing each other's girls and of course despising our opponents' successes to the fullest.

This was war, there was always a lot of competition and the one who one summer was your ally, the next became a bitter rival. This was done a lot by "el matador" and because of his betrayals we could not beat the leader on more occasions.

And if we fought and despised each other, let alone what we thought of everyone else. We laughed at them, we saw them as fools and we felt so superior, so superior, that even if they came to talk to us, we tried to keep this interaction as brief as possible, because we did not even consider them worthy of talking to us.

All this happened only in my summer resort, in my city Lugo without this extreme competitiveness, with much friendlier friends, I established a reign of terror in the years 92 and 93, which I still remember as powerful more than 30 years later.

What do we learn here?

- That if it is already difficult for an inexperienced young man to flirt, to get together with characters that do nothing but create tension and harm, does not benefit you in any way, and that you should go out with satisfactory partners or go out by yourself.
- That you have to be boastful and cocky but not arrogant and contemptuous.
- That good alliances give good results and bad alliances give bad results.
- That you can't really give your best if you're not in a pleasant environment.
- That even in a hostile environment, the immense dedication makes you advance.

This summer resort was a tough place to learn, the least positive thing were these fellow students who really made interacting with the girls less enjoyable.

In a real hell, where every night someone would hit on me, and then you had to put up with their scorn, I became hardened.

This helped me to separate myself from harmful people and only hang out with people who validated me. As soon as I eliminated these characters, I started to flirt a lot more, to feel more powerful and to enjoy myself a lot more.

First reign of terror.
Flashes of Fucking power.

What I described in the previous chapter occurred only in the summer city during 1992, 1993, 1994, 1995, 1996 and 1997, but for most of the year what I will now describe was happening

Now back to 1992 in my usual city, Lugo, while I was with this first girlfriend. For some time now I had not been feeling very well, as I felt that she bored me terribly, she did not seem to me neither fun, nor was I in tune with anything she thought, she had become a girl, bland, boring and even depressive, and although she was a wonderful person, she really bored me and I did not value her very much in these final stages.

At that time I met a group of friends and I had a great time drinking wine and laughing, and this really got me going.

It also happened that a friend told me that he fucked girls without being a boyfriend and without being anything of them. This left me in shock and angered me for swallowing the prudishness of the girlfriend, whom I had a hard time convincing to have sex. I felt like an idiot, and I wanted to put things right by fucking all of them from that moment on.

One day just like that, I really saw the light. I was listening to music, and it inspired me. I understood a hidden, mystical meaning behind the lyrics and I knew it was a sign. I felt transported, like someone who takes a pill and finally sees reality. It took 22 years to have this revelation, but this would change me forever and it was like an awakening. Suddenly, I felt different. The lyrics of the song inspired me and I felt much more bad, much more shameless, I felt an immense power, I knew that my formal stage was over and that now I was going to be bad, flirty, cocky and boastful and I felt fucking great.

After feeling the fucking power for the first time I changed my behavior to exactly how I had been feeling, and not caring about the consequences of my dirty tricks, I dedicated myself to pick up every hot girl I saw there in my own city.

I hooked up with two very pretty girls with enormous ease and one of them persevered a lot.

Now back to the summer resort where there was so much competition. It was 1992 and the O.L.P. had just been founded.

I went to my summer resort determined to succeed, there I tried and tried and tried and nothing came out, despite feeling so attractive and with so much desire, I did not flirt. Finally there was a day that I became demoralized and I thought that I would not flirt anymore, that it was impossible, because I had been 20 days entering girls without stopping, on the beach, on the street, at night, it was an exhausting and unsuccessful dedication. I must have had more than ten consecutive failures with girls I could not get to pick up. Girls to whom I dedicated effort to get nothing. I dedicated myself so much those days that I was exhausted, and sunk by the failure, I said that I was quitting, that I had failed, that I resigned myself to be a failure and that I would return to be formal with the girlfriend.

A week after this sad moment, the girls I went in with literally started coming to me. One came looking for me and asked me to meet her, her friend and a bunch of others. Suddenly I was fucking these two friends secretly almost every day, and I made a record number of hookups that was never broken again. It was the matador who generously introduced me to these girls, and thanks to this I finally started, and I had a legendary summer, fucking hot and devoted girls, literally fucking them in the ass and doing everything imaginable from the beginning, with all the fucking power.

I believe that in the end I would have been the same without this help, because the dedication made me get closer and closer to tuhe triumph.

Here with so much stress and so much competition I could not impose my beauty at ease, because they were also great handsome and diminished this advantage, I was weakened because I still did not have other weapons as powerful as this one.

Then I returned to my city of habitual residence Lugo very grown up, and there, without competition, I established a reign of terror. Every night I went out and collected my pieces, which were of the highest quality.

One night, with a brutal power and punch, I hooked up with several of them that same night. I hit on the ones I liked, and I hit on all their friends too, and their sisters, there was no girl left indifferent to me. Suddenly the power retained in these years with girlfriend was unleashed in a brutal way, and really here I reached the maximum level. I had no rival, no fear, no remorse. I didn't have all the knowledge, but I had the power, and this was a fucking massacre.

This reign of terror lasted almost all of '92 and all of '93.

Here I was brilliant and I felt like a great champion, I made a record of leagues in '93 that took ten years to beat, I was totally in the market and with a good head, something that later would not continue like that.

In '93 I hooked up with a friend of my girlfriend, I met her and that day I felt bad and libidinous and I thought -those tits are mine- and soon, not after months like with the girlfriend, soon, I was sucking and kneading them. I did great but great masteries. The biggest one was that I fucked the girlfriend of a guy I admired for being handsome and a flirt, a guy I considered the only one superior to me. Moreover, this girl was with me for many months, and so, fucking the girlfriend of the one I considered superior, I no longer saw anyone superior. This man was a security guard and had a gun, but I didn't mind risking my life to fuck this beautiful, big-assed girl. I was aware that he was a big bastard and by far the best in my fucking city.

So boastful and cocky was he that he was afraid of nothing.

One day I met my ex-teacher whose girlfriend I had fucked and who was left without her because of me. I saw him and thought -no big deal-.

He came to talk to me very friendly, he said that he was no longer dating the girl he was with and that he had found out that she was cheating on him. I told him, "But do you know who she is? And he said no.

We went for a few beers and we were talking about girls in a friendly way. And I told him that I had been fucking one and I told him about my fucks with his girlfriend and he laughed and was having a great time with me and he invited me for beers and everything. He invited me for beers and everything. Great guy!

Is this or isn't this from a teacher? I did this when I was 23. This was Jauja compared to my summer place.

I affirm that anyone from any city in Spain, no matter how much of a flirt he might be in his city, if he had gone out with the PLO, he would have been, not defeated, but humiliated by any of us.

Here in Lugo without rival, imposing my little dictatorship, I had the girls of the city surrendered at my feet.

I went out with another one as happy as a new girlfriend all over the city center, without caring if anyone saw me. I hooked up with another gorgeous girl, with whom I was having sex for hours and hours every night. At this time, I reached for a couple of years the maximum level in terms of results, and I also had a very good head, but there were still hidden weaknesses that came to light later. But we can say that in terms of power, I reached the maximum at the age of 22 and 23.

Also in my city I hooked up with one of that gang I hung out with, which gave me a strong high, because she was one that I liked a lot in the past, and for me it was something very important. Here I applied the fucking power and twisted reality, because I really didn't have much chance, but with the mastery of angles and distances that I was beginning to develop, and above all feeling the fucking power, I hooked her and she succumbed to her own surprise. Her boyfriend found out about this, who was also a half delinquent. I gave it my all and came out the winner and nothing happened to me.

What do we learn here?

- To feel the fucking power. To do this we will pay intense attention to something, especially empowering songs that we didn't realize before what they were really saying.
- That it is possible to succeed even when knowledge is at its rudiments.
- That dedication pays off.
- That being pissed off because what you think you deserve doesn't materialize, makes you go all out.
- Triumph always comes even if you stop if you did things right before.
- That you can be a master very soon.
- That you can hide your old self and create a much better one.
- That you have to believe in yourself and have faith.
- That you have to be bold.
- That one should be unconcerned about the risks.
- To be defiant in the face of danger.
- That you have to be able to be proud of it and boast about it.
- That if you think you are the best, you will become the best.

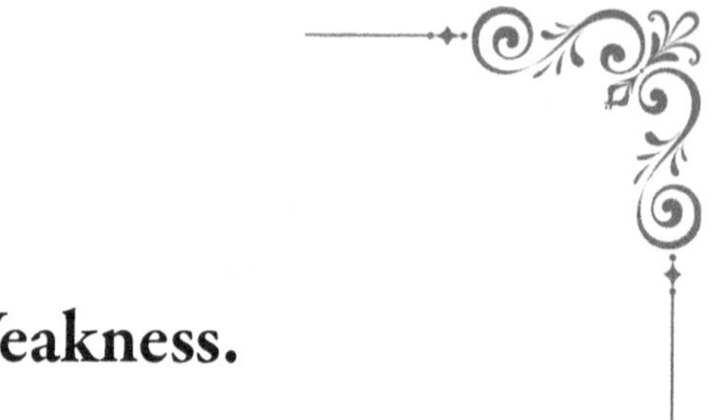

Weakness.

After a lot of playing the scoundrel, after reaching the fucking summit, I was very sure that this would always be the case. He had already broken up with his girlfriend so as not to hurt her anymore and everything was going perfect.

But one day I saw her and I remembered again the sensations of the beginning with her, this tormented me and made me fall apart completely, I felt terrible, I felt sorry to lose that beautiful love we had and I wanted to feel again what I felt at the beginning with her.

She, after much insistence came back to me briefly, but not at all convinced, and finally, she left me. I was totally dejected, sad and sorry for my wrongdoings, I felt very bad, ashamed of what I had done and wishing to return to the path of the good guy.

When a relationship breaks up you can get out in two ways:

With illusion to meet girls, have a good time, and not wanting to enter more in a relationship like this. So this is a very good breakup.

The opposite can also happen, that you think it was your fault, that you are sorry, that you are screwed and that as soon as you get out of that relationship you want to look for another one to redeem yourself, to be good, to go back to that idyllic love. This is the worst possible way out, the one that will cause terrible suffering, and this is what happened to me. After this first love I was left with remorse and softer than ever, soft looking for love again, feeling bad and guilty, in this state I was the perfect victim for any bad woman to fuck me alive.

It is unbelievable that after the wonders I did I was weakened like this, this was because I had not yet destroyed my old self, I had only locked it in my head and replaced it with the new one, but it was still there to fuck up my life and with this reencounter the old self came out again.

I think I was too young and I was this new me too recently built, so as soon as I exposed myself to the source of my weakness, the girlfriend, it broke my creation.

What do we learn here?

- That you should never feel guilty about ending a relationship, or this weakness will cause you to behave too kindly in the next one and they will abuse it.
- That you don't know how strong your new self is until you expose it to what weakens it.

Second girlfriend. Love sorrow as an imbecile.

Now after this first girlfriend I was no longer so happy, I was no longer all happy, I had really suffered for the first time in my life, this made me angry and frustrated. This frustration was growing, but so was the desire to find another nice girl.

What happened to me was horrible, but in the long run, the best thing that happened to me in life, because after much suffering, I finally became tough because of it. It so happened that I met another girl who was very nice and who I liked, and I had the misfortune to succeed and go out with her.

I who was already a bastard and a master, I wanted to restrain myself and be good. I was sad about losing the first girlfriend and I promised myself that I would be good to this second one.

This girl was very different from the first one and that got me excited, she was super crazy, fun, partying and outgoing, and I loved that in principle. She was also very hot and was, unlike the first one, very charismatic, talkative, and fun. As soft as I was, I succumbed completely to her enormous charms and threw myself into the relationship.

The problem was that this girl was neither sweet nor affectionate, nor as good as the other one, the only thing she cared about was partying, much more than being with me. At first I went with her to her countless parties, but I did not feel good, she did not pay enough attention to me, I felt unappreciated, sad, unrequited, and sometimes I even felt like she had too much in her life.

I restrained myself from counterattacking the numerous rebuffs he made to me, I was still there wandering around putting up with his nonsense, being needy and dependent.

But there were fights and arguments more and more frequently, and one day he got tired of me and left me.

After a year of being a jerk, suffering like never before in my life, trying to feel love and feeling nothing but sadness, loneliness and disappointment, she repaid me for this kindness with her low appreciation for me during the relationship, and finally with abandonment.

I was so bad that I completely transformed into a bad bad guy whose goal was to get revenge on her.

This girl wasn't bad at all, I don't think she was even bad, she was just cold and it wasn't her fault she was like that either, deep down, deep down, she was pretty good, but she made you mad as hell.

What do we learn here?

- That you do not enter into any relationship in a melancholic state or wanting to make up for something from the past.
- That your new girlfriend is not going to console you for what you did in the past.
- That you have to start cheerful and carefree any relationship.
- That on the path of the master you can stray for years on end, dominated by old beliefs that weaken you.
- That to be cold and hard, you must first be warm and soft.
- That in suffering is forged the determination not to suffer any more.
- That no one, not even your girlfriend will understand you, or help you in what is important to you.
- That you don't trust anyone especially your own girlfriend.

Second girlfriend. My conversion into a psychopath.

After she left me after putting up with everything, then I not only recovered my work, my bastard and flirtatious self, but I made it a lot worse. Shortly after leaving him she came back to me because despite everything, she must have liked something, or she had some hidden goodness and she was remorseful for what she had done to me.

But the me I had known no longer existed, I had already transformed into the bastard me, and now I would make him pay for all his scorn. This would be the most bastard version of my whole life.

There wasn't a day that went by that I didn't think she was a bad person who deserved all my hate and meanness.

I punished severely and cheated on her with dozens and dozens for years, as I resumed my career at 26, but this time being a real psychopath, for not only did I not regret anything, but I enjoyed my wickedness and got sadistically excited making her suffer. I went on a rampage with her.

I was half-madly devoted to despising her, humiliating her and making her suffer, and I succeeded completely. She behaved infinitely better with me, but I did not slacken the punishment one iota, and she suffered it for four long years.

It was not right what I did, because I hurt her too much, but at that moment it was what I felt. Here I didn't care much about the ones I was hitting on, but the revenge I was taking was what I liked the most.

By the way, I fucked and hooked up a lot.

These times, although I flirted a lot, were dark times, where the excess of meanness was just that, an excess. In the end, the few times I saw her, she behaved well with me, but even with that, I didn't let up. I was furious.

Many times she didn't hear from me for several days, I hung up the phone, or I didn't pick it up, or I fucked and went off to fuck someone else. I left her several times, I had other girlfriends, I even went out with several at the same time besides her. I said no to everything and she ended up saying yes to everything, and suffering because of my incredible hardness.

Finally, one night when the girlfriend had called me to go out and I said no, I got a call from a big-ass blonde who had hit on me and I went out with her. On a street I ran into the girlfriend as I was grabbing this chick, by the way much more stunning than she was. She saw me, screamed, and ran away.

And so went this bride and she was free of my sadism.

I, like with the other one, had a little slump, but very little, I called her but she never took my call and after feeling bad for a few days for being so, so, bad, in a short time I thought, better, let her go!

After so much hatred, one day I found her and I asked her forgiveness for all the bad things I had done and she forgave me, and so I calmed my bad conscience and felt better. That day she came close to coming back to me. She was about to sleep with me when she already had another boyfriend, but luckily there was very little time and when I told her to sleep with me she said she didn't have time and it was true. She wanted to. And so by pure luck I avoided falling into that trap again, which was not good for her or for me.

Leaving a girlfriend is good, losing a girlfriend you loved dearly is the best thing in your life. It hurts like hell, but it frees you from weakness and puts you back in the market where you should have always been.

After this terrible experience, I appeased the psychopath I had created and was at the perfect point of age, experience, evil and wisdom, to set up another great reign of terror in Santiago. This reign was much more powerful, cruel and ruthless than the previous one.

What do we learn here?

- There is no point in wanting to be good again when you have already programmed yourself to be bad.
- That it's not worth putting up with things you don't like about a girl.
- That revenge is not worth pursuing.
- That it is not worth it neither to suffer the rebuffs, nor to torture.
- That it is better to go your way and leave the girls who give problems. Because by being good you get nothing good from them and by being bad you do them excessive harm that they no longer deserve.

Today I wish the best to that poor girl who suffered my greatest follies, follies that came from bad feelings, from weakness, from the desire for revenge. Madnesses that then turn against you and you feel excessively bad.

The hardest thing to do is to make yourself respected and not to tolerate their abuses. If you do not achieve this, leave them without contemplation and never give in to their pleas.

The best harshness is not to punish or take revenge, the best harshness is to leave them and not care about them anymore, because they failed you, they don't deserve any chance since they didn't behave well with you.

In this case I liked myself too much, learn this and don't be a freak like I was. Free yourself and move forward.

Second reign of terror. Sweeping.

Now I unleashed all the fucking power, cleared my head of resentment and suffering and behaved in a much more positive, cheerful and happy way. Losing my girlfriend was wonderful and I enjoyed myself much more than before. At this time it was the year 2000 and I was 30 years old and I started to flirt and fuck much more frequently. In addition, exercising a very powerful domain, being coveted and valued by the women of my city.

At this time, I met a man who was a great seducer, "the Frenchman", and my alliance with him yielded spectacular results, on a level far superior to my previous alliances in my summer resort.

With this man, not one, not two, but three levels higher than before, and really incredible things were done that to count them all would require a book of a thousand pages.

The Frenchman and I were the masters of the city, and we made summers of records from '99 to 2005. It really was so much power that we were completely out of our minds. I used to say the phrase "i love this game" referring to how much I loved to flirt. We called ourselves the fucking masters.

In those years there was a crazy and sexual frenzy that I will relate later. There would be a lot to tell, if I start to tell the most outstanding adventures I would put here pages and pages and that is not what I want. Besides, that's what my secret work is for.

The teaching of all this is that, when you leave behind the softness and also the extreme hardnesses that do not bring you anything either, and you simply go out to enjoy, freed from unsatisfactory relationships, it is then when you give your maximum, you are yourself and you enjoy more than ever.

Now I loved my life and developed a personality similar to that of the first stage of great power in my former city of residence, Lugo, without resentment and without bullshit, I simply dedicated myself to enjoy.

There are three cities Lugo where I lived until 93, Santiago from 93 to now and Benicasim my summer resort where I went from 80 to 97.

This was a great time, I'm talking about the year 2000 onwards in Santiago, in which although I entered into small relationships, I quickly left, because I no longer believed in any love. I was simply with some girls that I liked a little more and I spent more time with them, but I knew that sooner or later they were going to give problems and they were going to leave me, or I was going to sacrifice them.

There is always a little stumble because you are not immune to his charms, but the damage suffered was minimal. He was living by and for the market, he was cold and hard on the inside and shameless and charming on the outside.

As a result of all this, a little girlfriend that I had for a while materialized. This girlfriend despite being physically one of the best, I did not value her much, nor did I care too much. So as I had my head with everything working at 100%, she did not give any problem and gave a portentous sexual performance, to the point of being able to say that it was already a totally porn relationship, because she was very devoted and, or was, or seemed a nymphomaniac, and what a performance she gave!

What do we learn here?

- That when we let go of grudges and unsatisfactory relationships, we develop our full power and seduce happily and joyfully.
- As a result of all this power, amazing girls appear who give

themselves to you in body and soul (especially in body), and you reach very high levels of sexual vice, which I will describe in the next chapter.

Enjoying a
Nymphomaniac.

What was left of the initial good guy? Well, nothing anymore. This original personality was left for occasional moments with exceptionally good girls. Now I knew how to measure, I knew when to reward and when to punish without overdoing it, and I found the balance between good and evil.

In the way of the master not everything is suffering, there are great enjoyments, and now at this moment, I was going to become a sexual master by fucking the craziest and hottest woman I met, a woman who really had no limits.

In order not to go on too long, I will tell you the most important and hot facts.

I nicknamed this girlfriend, who lasted about eight months, "Chochita" because of her pretty pink pussy.

The first day I already slept with her at her house, I fucked while her father was banging on the door because he knew she was there with someone, and while her father was banging, I fucked his daughter joyfully without giving a shit about anything anymore. I was totally uninhibited.

I enjoyed their luxury villa with pool very often, enjoyed their meals and the excursions we took.

Once while her parents were leaving in the car, they were leaving the garage and she leaned out the window to see them off. I pulled down her bikini from behind and while she was there to see them off I put my cock in her and started to fuck her while she was talking to her parents. They could not see me because I was further back as she put her ass back, and so she said goodbye.

Within ten minutes every day I saw her I was fucking her, often at her request. I always fucked once, twice, or three times, usually twice, but when I was with her all day three times, and I saw her practically every day. I fucked more with her in eight months than with others in years.

I didn't even know what to do to her anymore, I had fucked her in the ass, I had cum on her face and then she had gone for a walk with the cum on the street. I had stuck my big toe in her pussy, I had given her handjobs, blowjobs, tit-fucking, I had fucked her in her father's car. I had cum on her face with my sunglasses on and had sunbathed afterwards like that. One night I fucked her six times. Full on. She never said no to any proposal.

The culmination of all this was that I created the rule that every time I got in the car, she had to suck my cock all the way until I cum, and so we did for the eight months that the relationship lasted. I traveled very happy being sucked by this beautiful blonde with green eyes.

And although I did all these things I didn't feel any love attachment to her, and finally I got bored with all this fucking and left her.

She, who thought she was the most beautiful in town and the most attractive, ended up being dumped and on top of that she was hurt for losing me. I left her for someone even prettier, less crazy, sweeter and more attractive.

What do we learn here?

- That knowing everything about sex from so much practice you do makes you more powerful and gives you more confidence.
- That from so much enjoyment you end up with sexual addiction, and that way you are even more motivated to continue with the addiction.

Insignificant love affairs.

I think at age 31 I reached a peak of power that from that time until age 43 was very powerful.

I left the nymphomaniac girlfriend and picked up a prettier one that I liked much more, and for a little while I felt weakened again and falling in the clutches of love, but this would only last me a month and a half or two. I immediately saw her many flaws, her nonsense, her bullshit and I began to think she was a child, as she really turned out to be. And after enjoying this beautiful girl I was liberated. I had a little bit of a bad time at the end, but nothing that I wouldn't get over in two or three days.

Then I hooked up with another one who invited me to a city far away in Spain and paid for my plane fare. And that's how I lived, going out with short-term girlfriends who invited me and took me around. I also had others who fucked me on the side, went to private pools, came to pick me up in BMWs, and it was as if I was the prize and they competed to be with me. I also had a very busty and busty fucker who gave me tremendous blowjobs and to whom I assigned that function.

Anyway, I don't want to be here telling all my stories, there were many more things to tell, I'm only going to put what I think can help you to become a teacher, so instead of bragging and going into details, I'm going to tell you the teaching of this chapter.

Here we learn that

- Even if you go out with someone and you really think you are formal, you can't be formal even if you want to, because you are already so into the vice of fucking everyone, that it is impossible to be faithful to any of them.

- We also learn that after so much practice you become hard, you don't give a shit if they lose their girlfriends, if they get angry, or whatever. There comes a time when you almost don't suffer, you see them as silly and capricious and you have no desire to please them.

And so, valuing them in their right measure, pulling them very low, and sometimes scoring them above zero, knowing that it is practically the same to lose them because there are many more, and also better, and that you get them easily and quickly, you get to the top. You start fucking girls on the first day and here you reach almost the maximum level.

Now I will tell you some more things that are left but practically this is almost all you need.

Loneliness.

There comes a moment in the path of the master in which you can't stand them anymore, you are no longer willing to go through any relationship or swallow with their nonsense, whims and bullshit. At this moment you prefer your solitude and it is when you have the best time and the best you are.

Being alone you are never short of women, because you have all the time in the world to dedicate to flirt and flirt without getting into any relationship. You flirt and make it clear that you don't want anything serious with them. This is what makes them most loyal to you, so they all want to go out with you and accept your demands. They try to have you fucking like lionesses, but they don't succeed, and one after another they are conquered, made little attention, and finally either they leave alone, or you abandon them, because you don't want to put up with anything at all.

And so mass production is being made, an industrial production that is what differentiates you from all the others who waste their time in absurd relationships, which bring them nothing but pain and dissatisfaction.

When the matador came here in my heyday, he took such a beating that he was even embarrassed and said that he had never seen greater power and mastery in his life than I had in Santiago.

In your loneliness you won't have many friends either because: they will either be envious, or they won't keep up with you, or they won't understand you, and besides, you won't have time because you will always be going from woman to woman. So enjoy this loneliness, which is not loneliness at all, because you are more accompanied than ever.

What do we learn here?

- When you have come to the conviction that you are better off alone than with any girlfriend, you have reached a very high point on the path of the master and this will be super rewarded by the market.
- Nothing attracts a woman more than a man she can't hold on to.
- Reaching this lonely and fucking state is hard, because before you suffered in relationships, and the weariness and tiredness of these makes you become colder and harder than ever, and at the same time more irresistible.
- When you get to the top, everyone pays homage to you and if they don't, you don't care.

Being invited.

So independent, cool, carefree, and attractive, you attract lots of girls who bid for your services. Some offer sex easily, others offer sex too but think that's not enough and also offer money. These wealthy girls will try to buy you off by inviting you to everything, taking you on trips and paying for everything themselves, being very nice and always available to you without any protests.

If you reach very high levels, not only will you take advantage of them, but you will reach a point where you will despise them, tell them that they are not going to buy from you, and that their invitations are not worth it.

You'll leave them abandoned, you'll give them very fat rebuffs, and they'll still be there like gawking, some of them for the rest of their lives or at least more than 20 years, until finally one day they get tired of waiting to be reciprocated and go off with some fool, and finally they leave you alone, and you can get rid of them and their harassment.

These girls are obsessed with you and they are willing to let you pick up all their friends, have girlfriends, ignore them, and they are always there for you.

What do we learn from this?

- That when you become cold hard and independent, some of them go crazy and fall unconditionally surrendered. This state can last them for many years, and more than occasional lovers, because you don't even want them for that, they seem like your admirers. If on top of that you do not value them at all as it usually happens, they will admire you and they will not leave even if you fuck their friends, or whatever you do to them. Here you will have reached monstrous levels of mastery.

Dictatorship.

Once you reach dictatorship you have reached the maximum reasonable level, but you can still get to a higher level by doing really crazy things. Dictatorship is knowing that you are the hottest guy in town and thinking that there is no one better than you, at least of those you know. You live a real porn actor's life, fucking too often and putting your life at risk, because of so much hustle and bustle, and so much physical wear and tear.

Dictatorship is to dominate with an iron fist not only your relationships, but your city. Every day you go out you know they are out there wanting to meet you, numerous attractive girls, who soon become part of the productive process, coming in and out of our lives, without making any dent in our toughness, or causing us any pain.

The dictatorship is to be a master of flirting, who is almost not even happy about his victories, this is not true, you are always a little happy, but you are less happy, so many girls that you flirt, so much dominance, so much success. There comes a time when we can say that, despite the problems that some of them give, they are very small compared to those of girlfriends. You are living a paradise on earth from which you should never leave.

What do we learn here?

- That at the end of the master's path is paradise and that this paradise can last as long as you keep your capacities at the maximum in mentality. If you achieve this, only the physical, as it wanes, will gradually take you away from being the dictator.

- The dictatorship is to reach the top and do legendary feats. When everyone knows you and you have a reputation as a flirt, many are attracted precisely because of this reputation.
- The dictatorship is not being able to attend to so many that you have and really doubt if you will be doing well or if you should loosen up so as not to die from so much fucking.

Sex addiction.

That's right, by the end of the master's journey you become a sex junkie and you have to get your fix, practically daily, or you get nervous and anxious.

If you have many girls to sleep with at the same time and without any commitment with any of them, then you will fuck like never before and you will be totally addicted. This is not good, it is very good, here you reach your maximum splendor and after this you will have to lower the demand a little because this is already excessive and you can really die. Besides, it is a lot of stress so many women, so after a while giving your best and seeing death up close, you end up getting scared and in the end you lose your mind and go on to do other things more fun and crazier, but less tiring.

We learn all this here.

- We learn that this period of maximum fucking can only be maintained for a few years, and then you must rest, or something very serious can really happen to you.
- Most of them can't stand such wear and tear and relax afterwards by doing other less strenuous activities, and since there's nothing left to do after that, you go full circle and go back to being a bad boy but looking semi-good.

BDSM.

If you have a lot of girls to fuck you will end up doing it rough, because they themselves will ask you to do it, they will tell you to treat them hard, or you see that this excites them and so you do it. You go out of your mind from so much fucking and you become half crazy and fuck like a porn actor in a rage. Others, even more vicious, tell you directly to hit them while you are fucking them, or to talk dirty to them.

In short, you will end up being a S&M master sooner or later. After that, you'll hardly get turned on at all because it's much wilder than normal sex.

You become completely envy and lower the production, because you no longer say anything about fucking with girls in the normal way, but these will become your slaves, the ones that will give you more satisfaction, and the ones to whom you will dedicate more preference. Then, due to these perversions, the production will decrease and you will relax the wear and tear.

What do we learn here?

- That sadomaso-style fucking satisfies you much more.
- That this lowers your production.

Power peaks.

The peaks of my power happened in 92, 93, 99, 2000, 2001, 2002, 2003, 2005, 2006, 2007, 2009, 2010, 2011, then a strong drop and it would not be until 2018 and especially 2019 when it would return to stand out. This goes in waves and in these years of power peaks double, triple, and even quadruple figures were made than in other weaker years.

What do we learn from all this?

- We learn that in the good years when the wave comes, when you are with all your power, you do a lot more than in normal years and these years balance the bad years and make everything very positive.

Good years happen the more dedication you put into them, it's as simple as that, a great part of success is dedication. Whoever puts dedication, if he already has the wisdom, makes the records.

Relaxing.

Finally you end up a little tired, not from so much fucking, not from so much going out, not from so much partying and so many women; what happens is that physically and mentally you are exhausted, sometimes it is very stressful. If you find a woman who is hot, good at sex and spoiled with your adventures and conquests, a woman who plays dumb with your constant dalliances, then you slow down, calm down a bit and rest.

I'm not saying you're going to be formal, but you do become, at least, attached to her, and you give her quite a bit of importance. She thinks she has a boyfriend and you dedicate yourself to a much lesser extent to seduction, but you are still dedicated and you are quite happy, because you have a good girl and you also seduce.

What starts as something temporary to rest, often turns into something definitive and the seducer gradually fades away. That's why you can't get too comfortable or the game will end. You must always do it temporarily and just enough time to recover. This is how the careers of seducers who could not stop this end.

What do we learn here?

- That you have to rest from time to time, but be careful not to relax too much, because the temporary rest will end up being your tomb as a seducer if it lasts too long.
- That if you can avoid it better.

Waves.

In seduction and in general in everything in life, there are moments when everything goes smoothly, as if a wave of receptive women come to you, and then once it passes, there is a very empty time, in which, although you try even harder than during the wave, you get much less. You have to be attentive and surf all these waves that come to you.

If the wave comes then there will be moments of high production peaks and you will give preference to seduction, and if there are moments of shortage you give preference to this girl who relaxes you and calms you down. One girl is normal but it can also be several.

I recommend having the triad, at least 3 aunts.

When you enter advanced age, you are usually dedicating a small percentage of your time to seduction, because the market is also declining. So, at this time, you are not retired, but you are semi-retired, waiting for good offers. And this is how the seducer's life can end, each time surfing smaller and smaller waves and gradually retiring.

As soon as the wave arrives, you rarely, if ever, resist it and abandon your tranquility, and even if it is great, you break up with these women who reassure you and return again to intensive seduction.

There are several semi retreats and turns. It's like waves that come and go, and so enjoying the waves that are passing and enjoying the time voluntarily at low activity, the end of your days is coming.

As you are a champion, it happens that at very high ages women continue to circulate in your life, as it could not be otherwise.

What do we learn here?

- Even if your production drops, even if you are semi-retired, even if you dedicate yourself less because you no longer perform as you used to, you never retire completely and you are always eager to seduce, you always live for seduction, which you never give up during your whole life.

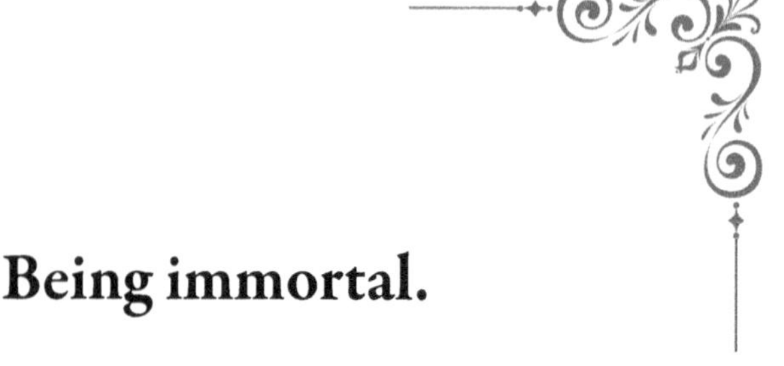

Being immortal.

After decades of enjoying yourself like a bastard, bragging about everything you have enjoyed, you go and tell people about it. You do this so that they can have access to your knowledge, also out of sheer cockiness and boastfulness, also so that at least it is known that you existed and that you made a different life than normal people do.

There are many people who do this, but some like me have done it to insane levels. I am very happy to be addicted to women, sex, adventure and excitement.

Through my books this knowledge will remain and people will know what my view of all this was. This gives you fame recognition and makes you immortal, so after all, even bragging about all my misdeeds, I think this gives me prestige.

I believe that I am helping many men to get out of a miserable life, a life based on paying obeisance to women who never correspond to them from a plane of equality, but rather from a position of superiority to them, whom they treat as their subordinates haughtily. It is for all these men, who are going to become real men again through these teachings, that I am motivated to write all this that I am writing.

What do we learn here?

- That in the end you like to be you, you brag about your conquests, you feel the fucking master and you are super proud of what you have done.

The meaning of everything.

The meaning of everything is to fulfill the divine function that was assigned to you at birth, because this is something you feel deep inside, you know that you were born for enjoyment, partying, and women.

The meaning of everything is to comply with the mission assigned to you, God wants it and is pleased with it.

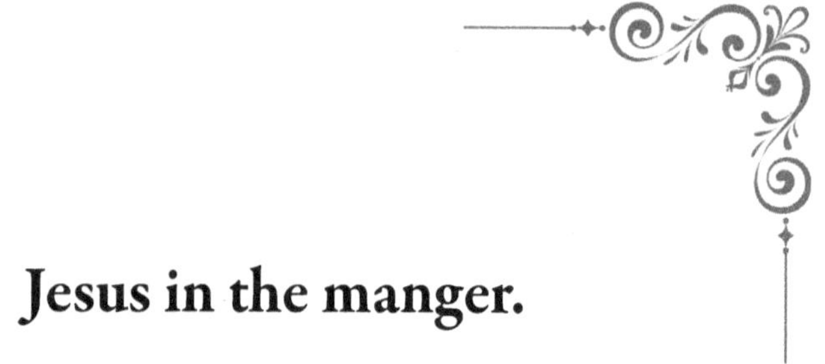

Jesus in the manger.

One day I heard a Christmas carol and it made me laugh. I was struck by a verse that said.

-And Jesus in the manger, he laughs, because he is joyful.

Jesus in the manger is a child who laughs because he is joyful. So should you be, whatever level you are at, and whatever you achieve, you should laugh because nothing matters since you are practicing and dedicating yourself, you are on the path of the master.

Looking at your whole life in perspective, you don't differentiate very well between the good times and the bad times, because everything seems good to you. Now I think that the times of gloom with horrible results and enormous suffering were just as satisfactory as the times of prosperity.

Both times were good, what happens is that when you are in the bad times, you don't realize that this is what you need to be able to get to the good times later.

In the end you selectively remember only the good moments and forget the bad ones. Now I think that it was the bad moments that made me powerful, because the good moments were the materialization of what I devised in my lousy moments, when I became hardened, determined, disciplined, and changed what was necessary.

Although it is true that the times of fucking like crazy are more enjoyable, one thing is a consequence of the other and everything is good.

Whatever happens to you, you have to be like Jesus in the manger, a child who laughs because he is joyful. Just like that, joyful for the sake of it. If you are like that, you will enjoy everything that happens to you. Even if you don't become a master in seduction, if you manage to be like Jesus in the manger who laughs because he is joyful, you will enjoy.

What we learn here

- You have to laugh, but working on the path of becoming a master, laughing at the bad moments because they are really not so bad, because you are already on the path to change what is happening to you.
- Laughing for the sake of it is a very happy person and that's fine and I think it's wonderful, but if you're not on the path to bettering yourself, that laughter will soon turn into tears.

Pleasing yourself even more.

And so I end this book, pleasing myself once again, boasting of my misdeeds, feeling proud of all my massacres, and warning that this is not over and that I intend to continue until the day of my death. And if I could request it, in my next reincarnation I would again request to be a seducer, as I believe I did before I was born, for this is the best life there is, far and away superior to all others.

Final summary.

The path of the master begins in childhood or adolescence and ends a little before death. The girls change, the age changes, but the spirit remains unchanged; and so through the decades, through your whole life, you go seducing women for the mere satisfaction of seducing them.

If you follow the master's path you will learn the seduction techniques that I haven't talked about here, but that's what my books "Master in seduction" and "JD Absolute seduction" are for. With them and with your incessant practice you will go from being a man who suffers, to an independent, happy and fucking tough guy.

Anyone can make it to the end of the master's path if they put firm determination into it. That is your great weapon, the dedication, the determination to persevere, to get up, to continue, far above any physique or ability.

The road has bumps, curves and dangers, the greatest dangers always come from love, and it is the same girls you conquer who also slow you down.

You owe it to the next one, you must think of that one who is alone, sad and bored, that one you don't know yet, but who needs you. Think of that woman and go out and look for her. That woman is not happy, she suffers. You remedy it and make her happy.

Dedicate yourself to your production, to continue turning sad, sexually apathetic, bored women into hot, joyful, happy, fun women.

You do good, you also do a little evil, but this results in a greater good, you serve society, you serve life and it is good, just and necessary.

Dark seduction is a secret weapon, something hidden that no one knows and that you know and use on very rare occasions. It is a knowledge that you learned while walking the path of the master, but that must remain a secret, waiting in case it is ever needed.

The path of the master is a path from pain to joy. From darkness to light.

To succeed in it, you don't have to reach the end, go where you want to go, everyone has their own goals and not everyone may want to go all the way. If you reach what you promised to reach, even if it is not the end, you will have succeeded too. I won't understand it but you will. ha ha.

Teammates come and go, rivals fall, time goes by. 40 years after you started, the one who remains is you, you are still in the game in search of new feats to increase your legend even more.

Yes, we are sick, yes, we are immature, childish, blah, blah, blah, blah, all you want, but how good it is like this!

And so, from deranged to deranged, I tell you, I know that there will be many who will follow my legacy, and inspired by it, will far surpass it.

The master's path is to go from feeling fearful, nervous, frustrated and sad, to feeling powerful, dominant, happy and boastful for all that has been achieved.

And so the boy who imagined being his hero ended up being his hero.

If the girls no longer remember you because of the long time that has passed, it doesn't matter, what matters is that it happened, that you were there, that you did your wonders. That will remain forever not only in your head, but also in the spirit of the books, and if someone reads them attentively, he will be able to feel all the sensations that I have told. Someone will be able to become a Master.

We do the girls a lot of good, we make them have a great time with us. The way of the master is to spread joy, a little love and a lot of fun.

The way of the master is to leave behind the softnesses and practice the hardnesses, but it is also to leave behind excessive hardness, for that hardness is actually weakness and harms us.

I congratulate myself also for these people of the future who will continue this wonderful, just, and pure life, the best life in the world, the life of the shameless and charming seducer.

One day, less and less distant, the path of the master will end in the imagination of an old man who returns to relive his adventures and to fantasize about new ones that will never come.

You can be the next master!

Let's play!
Let's fly!
Let's succeed!

Did you love *Master's Path*? Then you should read *How to Materialize What You Want With The Fxxxxxx Power*[1] by John Danen!

There is an infinite power in you to materialize what you most desire. Seduction meets the law of attraction and this book arises, a book that explains step by step how to activate and manifest this power, the Fucking power.

---

1. https://books2read.com/u/bPezvl

2. https://books2read.com/u/bPezvl

Also by John Danen

Seduction 5.0

S.A.X.

Chicas complicadas

Seducción 5.0

El libro del tonto

Macho Alpha

Macho alpha extracto

La seducción después de la pandemia

Terriblemente atractivo

Seducción 5.1

Sedução 5.1

How to be Cool and Attractive

Sedução. Avançada. X.

Garotas complicadas

¡Basta de ser buen chico! Sé un chico malo.

El método JD. El método de seducción de John Danen

El arte de agradarte a ti mismo

¡Basta ya de abusos! ¡Defiéndete!

Enought with the abuse! Defend yourself!

Máster en seducción

Las mujeres. El amor. Y el sexo.

Supera la dependencia emocional

Atrae mujeres con masculinidad

JD Absoluta seducción

El fracaso del amor

Entender a las mujeres

La vida del seductor sinvergüenza y encantador.

El arte de la dureza

Terrivelmente atraente

Deixe de ser um bom da fita! Seja um mauzão.

Superar a dependência emocional

A arte de se agradar

Pare o abuso! Defenda-se!

O fracasso do amor.

O método JD

Don´t Be a Good Boy! Be a Badass

Complicated girls

The Art of Pleasing Yourself

Duro y Sinvergüenza

Mestre en sedução

JD Method

The Failure of Love. The Trap of Serious Relationships

Master in Seduction

A. S. X. Advanced. Seduction. X

Women. Love. Sex

How to Become a Real Man. Be an Alpha Male

Attract Women with Masculinity

JD Absolut Seductión

Understanding Women

The Life of the Shameless and Charming Seducer.

The Art of Toughness

Tough and Shameless

Überwindung der Emotionalen Abhängigkeit

Maître en séduction

Schrecklich Attraktiv

Surmonter la Dépendance Émotionnelle

L'art de la dureté

Die Kunst der Zähigkeit

Hör auf, ein guter Junge zu sein, sei ein böser Junge
Assez D'être un Bon Garçon ! Sois un Mauvais Garçon.
Die Kunst, sich Selbst zu Gefallen
Dur et sans Vergogne
Hart im Nehmen und Schamlos
L'art de se Plaire à soi-Même
Das Scheitern der Liebe
L'échec de L'amour.
Meister der Verführung
Die JD-Methode
Maestro di Seduzione
Terriblement Attrayant
La Méthode JD
Capire le donne
Compreendendo as Mulheres
Comprendre les Femmes
Die Frauen Verstehen
Les Filles Compliquées
Komplizierte Mädchen
JD Séduction Absolue
La Vie du Séducteur Charmant et sans Vergogne
Les Femmes. L'amour. Et le Sexe.
Mâle Alpha
S.A.X.
V.F.X.
Donne. Amore. E il sesso.
Ragazze Complicate
Superare la Dipendenza Emotiva
Seduzione. Avanzata. X.
Dark Seducción
Il Fallimento Dell'amore.
Il Metodo JD
Alphamännchen

Atrair Mulheres com Masculinidade
Attirare le donne con la Mascolinità
Attirer les Femmes par la Masculinité
Mit Männlichkeit Frauen Anziehen
Frauen. Liebe. Und Sex.
L'arte di Piacere a se Stessi
Mulheres. Amor. E Sexo.
JD Seduzione Assoluta
JD Absolute Verführung
JD Sedução Absoluta
Das Leben des charmanten, schamlosen Verführers
Smettila di Fare il Bravo Ragazzo! Essere un Cattivo Ragazzo.
La Vita del Seduttore Affascinante e Spudorato
A Vida do Sedutor Encantador e sem Vergonha
Macho Alfa
Uomo Alfa
Séduction 5.0
Verführung 5.0
Seduzione 5.0
Duro e Senza Vergogna
Duro e Sem Vergonha
L'arte della Durezza
A Arte da Dureza
The Fool's Book
Das Buch der Dummköpfe
Il Libro dei Pazzi
O Livro do Tolo
Dark Seduction
Dunkle Verführung
Sedução Escura
Dark Seduction
Seduzione Oscura
Le livre du fou

Como materializar lo que deseas con el fxxxxx power

Como materializar o que você quer com o Fxxxxx Power

El ángel Sex-terminador

El seductor vampiro

O Vampiro Sedutor

Sex-Terminating Angel

The Vampire Seducer

How to Materialize What You Want With The Fxxxxx Power

El camino del maestro

Il vampiro seduttore

O camiño do mestre

La via del maestro

Der verführerische Vampir

Le sedusant vampire

Der Weg des Meisters

La voie du maître de la séduction

Master's Path

Come materializzare ciò che si desidera con il Fxxxxx Power

Wie Sie Ihre Wünsche verwirklichen können mit dem Fxxxxx Power

El método EDP

O método EDP

The EDP method

About the Author

Español.

Soy un hombre vividor y divertido que busca el lado bueno de las cosas siempre.

Mi experiencia es el campo de las relaciones personales y de la seducción. Por eso tras dedicarme larguísimas décadas a ello, quiero trasmitir mis conocimientos. Para que las nuevas generaciones tengan unos conceptos que les den una ventaja competitiva sostenible y poderosa en el campo del amor.

Quiero ayudarte a a conseguir tus metas.

Portugués.

Sou um homem animado, e divertido, que sempre procura o lado bom das coisas.

Minha experiência está no campo das relações pessoais e da sedução. É por isso que, após décadas de dedicação a ela, quero transmitir meus conhecimentos.

Quero ajudá-los a alcançar seus objetivos.

Inglés

I am a lively and fun man, who always looks for the good side of things.

My experience is in the field of personal relationships and seduction. That is why, after decades of dedicating myself to it, I want to pass on my knowledge. So that the new generations have concepts that give them a sustainable and powerful competitive advantage in the field of love.

I want to help you achieve your goals

Français Je suis un homme vif et drôle qui cherche toujours le bon côté des choses.

Mon expérience se situe dans le domaine des relations personnelles et de la séduction. C'est pourquoi, après m'y être consacré pendant des décennies, je veux transmettre mes connaissances. Pour que les nouvelles générations disposent de concepts qui leur donnent un avantage concurrentiel durable et puissant dans le domaine de l'amour.

Je veux vous aider à atteindre vos objectifs.